D1605393

The Zoo's
Who's Who

Penguins

Katie Franks

PowerKiDS
press™

New York

Published in 2015 by The Rosen Publishing Group, Inc.
29 East 21st Street, New York, NY 10010

First Edition

Editor: Jennifer Way
Photo Research: Katie Stryker
Book Design: Joe Carney

Photo Credits: Cover Elenarts/iStock/Thinkstock; p. 5 Volodymyr Goinyk/iStock/Thinkstock; p. 6 moodboard/Thinkstock; p. 9 Tomislav Konestabo/Shutterstock.com; p. 10 J.E. Mous/Shutterstock.com; p. 13 LMPphoto/Shutterstock.com; p. 14 Fuse/Thinkstock; p. 17 Purestock/Thinkstock; p. 18 Jörg Drews/iStock/Thinkstock; p. 21 Volodymyr Goinyk/Shutterstock.com; p. 22 diamant24/iStock/Thinkstock.

Library of Congress Cataloging-in-Publication Data

Franks, Katie.
  Penguins / by Katie Franks.
      pages cm. — (The zoo's who's who)
  Includes index.
  ISBN 978-1-4777-6472-5 (library binding) — ISBN 978-1-4777-6576-0 (pbk.) —
ISBN 978-1-4777-6577-7 (6-pack)
  1. Penguins—Juvenile literature. I. Title.
  QL696.S473F723 2015
  598.47—dc23
                            2013047660

Manufactured in the United States of America

CPSIA Compliance Information: Batch #WS14PK4: For Further Information contact Rosen Publishing, New York, New York at 1-800-237-9932

Contents

Penguins live in the southern half of Earth. There are about 20 kinds of penguins.

Crested penguins have feathers on their heads. Rockhoppers are crested penguins.

Emperor penguins are the largest penguins. They live in Antarctica.

9

Penguins have lots of feathers. Their feathers keep them warm in cold weather.

Penguins cannot fly. They have **flippers** instead of wings. Flippers help penguins swim.

13

Penguins have strong feet. Their feet have **claws**. Claws help them walk on ice.

A group of penguins is a **colony**. Penguins form colonies to have babies.

17

Penguins hold their eggs on their feet. They hold the eggs close to their bodies. This keeps the eggs warm.

Baby penguins are called chicks. Most penguins have one chick at a time.

Penguins are fun to see at the zoo. You can watch them swim and play.

23

WORDS TO KNOW

claws

colony

crested

flipper

WEBSITES

Due to the changing nature of Internet links, PowerKids Press has developed an online list of websites related to the subject of this book. This site is updated regularly. Please use this link to access the list: www.powerkidslinks.com/zww/peng/

INDEX